Octave
Scale Studies
for the Violin

Book One

by Cassia Harvey

CHP262

©2014 by C. Harvey Publications® All Rights Reserved.
www.charveypublications.com - print books & free sheet music blog
www.learnstrings.com - PDF downloadable books & chamber music

Octave Scale Studies for the Violin

Cassia Harvey

2

Octave Scale Studies for the Violin, Book One

3

Octave Scale Studies for the Violin, Book One

4

Octave Scale Studies for the Violin, Book One

5

6

Octave Scale Studies for the Violin, Book One

7

8

Octave Scale Studies for the Violin, Book One

9

10

Octave Scale Studies for the Violin, Book One

11

12

13

14

Octave Scale Studies for the Violin, Book One

15

©2014 C. Harvey Publications All Rights Reserved.

16

17

18

Octave Scale Studies for the Violin, Book One

19

20

Octave Scale Studies for the Violin, Book One

21

©2014 C. Harvey Publications All Rights Reserved.

22

Octave Scale Studies for the Violin, Book One

23

24

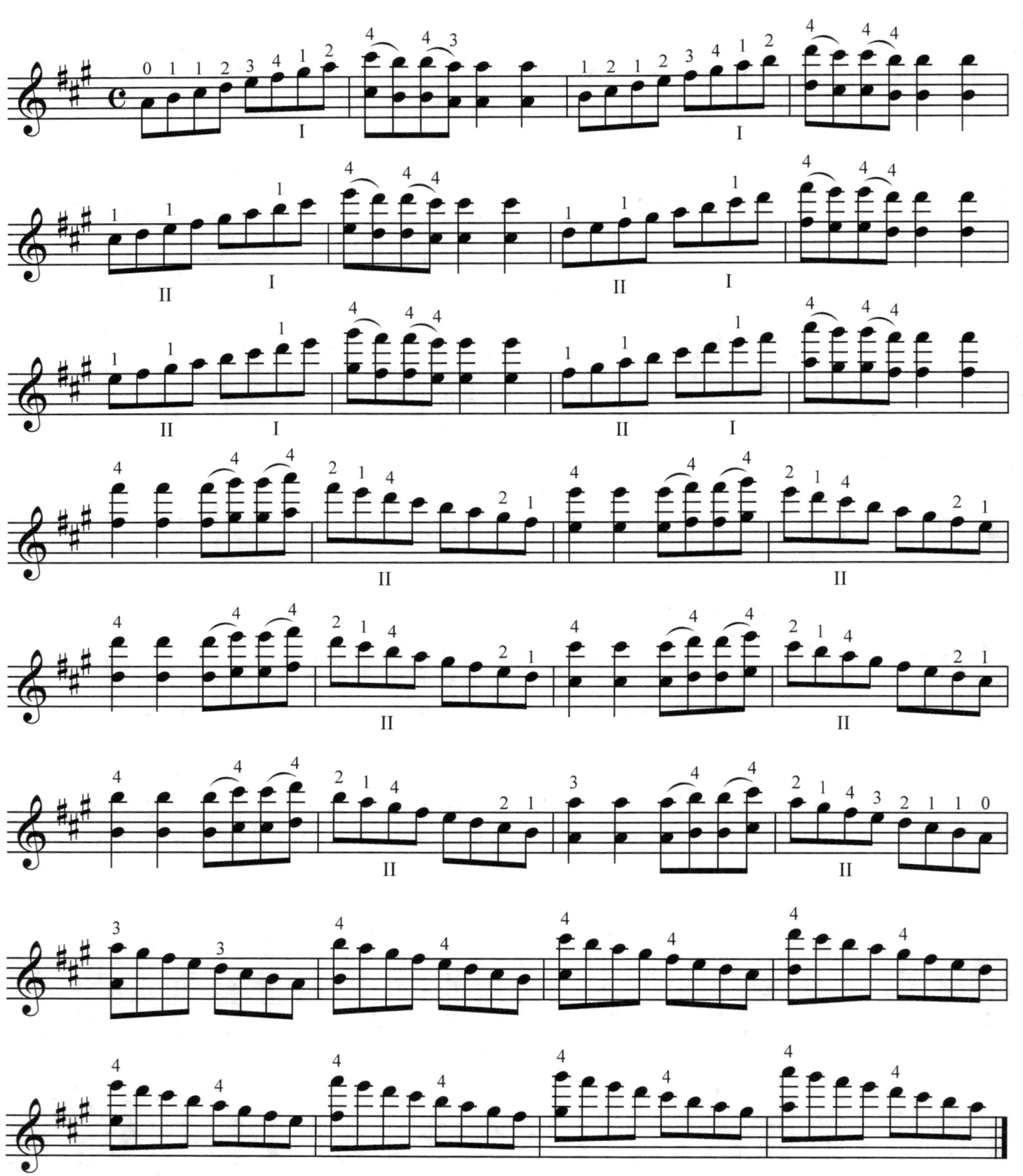

Octave Scale Studies for the Violin, Book One

25

Octave Scale Studies for the Violin, Book One

27

28

Octave Scale Studies for the Violin, Book One

29

30

available from www.charveypublications.com: CHP246

Fourth Position for the Violin

by Cassia Harvey

A. First Shifting on the A String

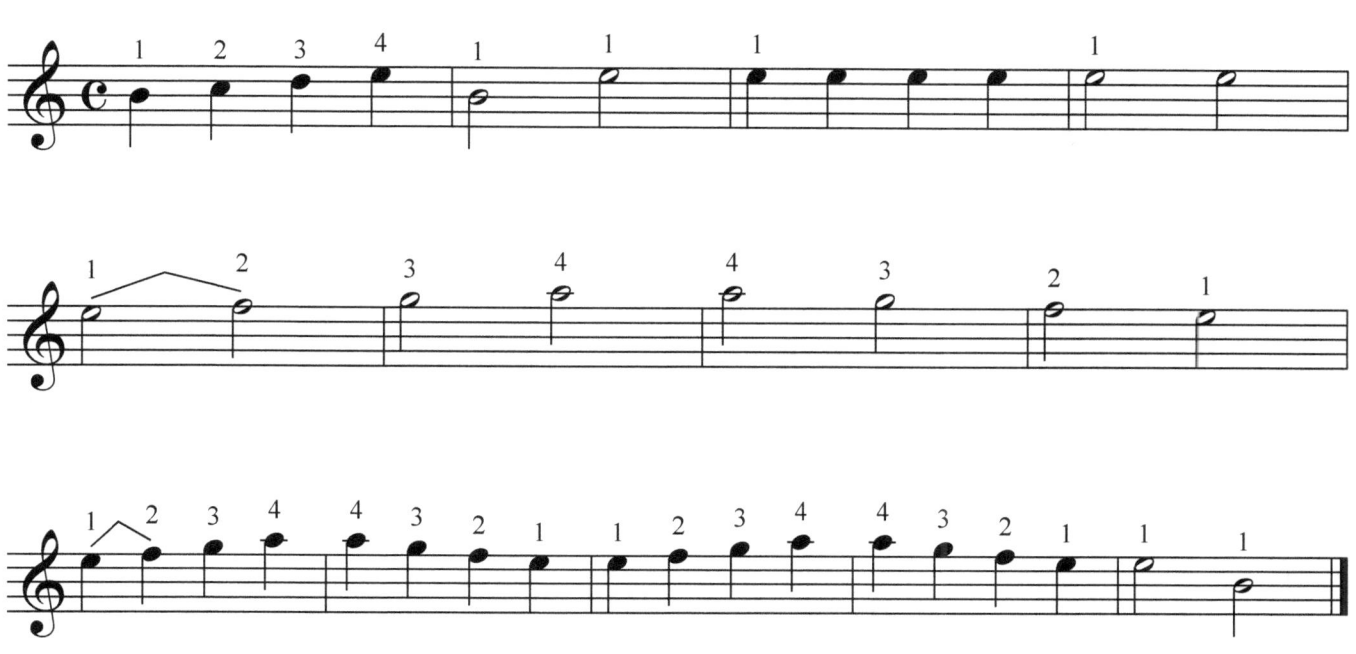

B. First Shifting on the E String

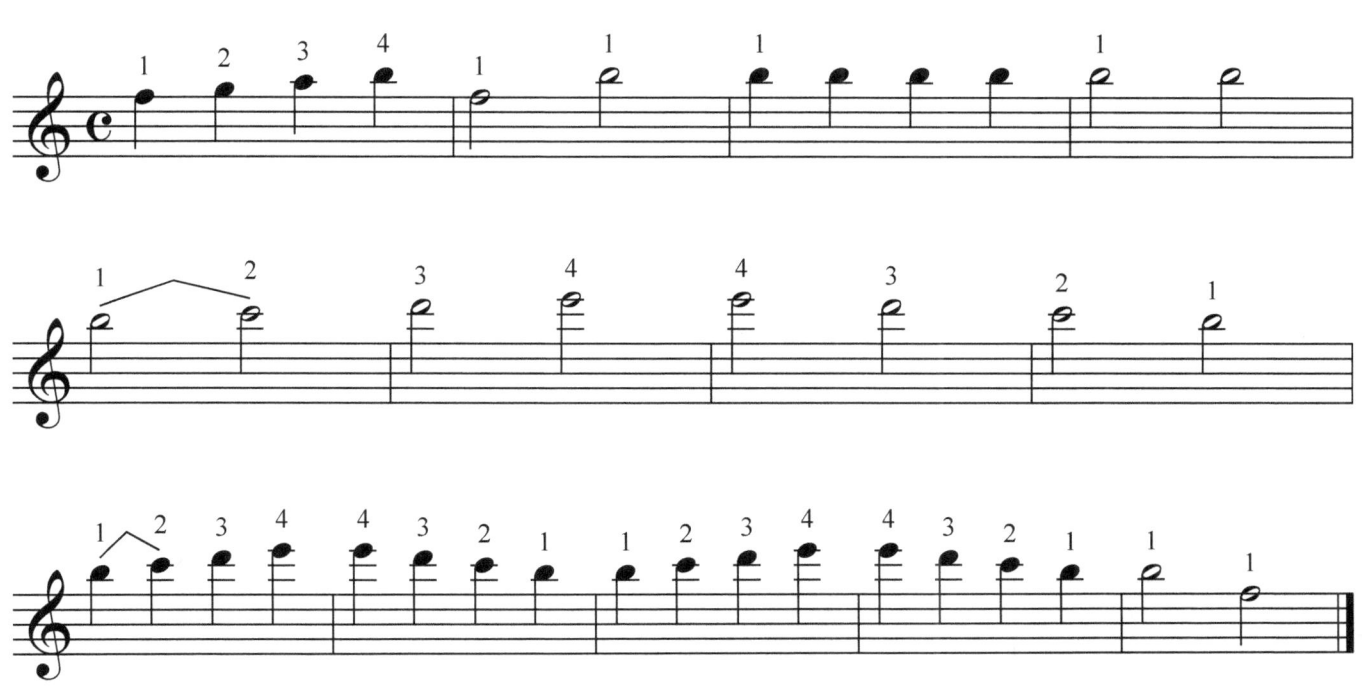

©2014 C. Harvey Publications All Rights Reserved.

www.ingramcontent.com/pod-product-compliance
Lightning Source LLC
Chambersburg PA
CBHW051430070526
44584CB00023B/3660